IMAGES
of America

SPOKANE PARKS

ON THE COVER: Children and adults find space among the trees at Franklin Park, located on Division Street between Queen and Nebraska Avenues. This park was purchased because of its location in the north-central part of the city and the beautiful woodland. The trees provide some shade, but many of the people enjoying the park are shaded from the sun with umbrellas. The image is a reminder of A *Sunday Afternoon on the Island of La Grande Jatte* by pointillist painter Georges Seurat. (Courtesy of Washington State Archives.)

IMAGES
of America

SPOKANE PARKS

Washington State Archives

ARCADIA
PUBLISHING

Copyright © 2023 by Washington State Archives
ISBN 978-1-4671-0947-5

Published by Arcadia Publishing
Charleston, South Carolina

Printed in the United States of America

Library of Congress Control Number: 2022948121

For all general information, please contact Arcadia Publishing:
Telephone 843-853-2070
Fax 843-853-0044
E-mail sales@arcadiapublishing.com
For customer service and orders:
Toll-Free 1-888-313-2665

Visit us on the Internet at www.arcadiapublishing.com

For those who love the great outdoors as a place to connect with nature and commune with those in the past who enjoyed the very same spot.

CONTENTS

ACKNOWLEDGMENTS

This book would not have been possible without the help of so many individuals and institutions. We will try to acknowledge them all and apologize if you were missed. Fulfilling this opportunity to highlight our collections east of the mountains could not have been possible without Steve Excell, former state archivist of the Washington State Archives, and Terry Badger, deputy state archivist. Special thanks to Dr. Larry Cebula for inspiring us with his never-ending charge to share history with the public. Riva Dean, former librarian of the Spokane Public Library's Northwest Room, the City of Spokane's Parks Department staff, and Anna Harbine and Alex Fergus of the Northwest Museum of Arts and Culture were also instrumental in helping us illustrate the vibrant history of Spokane's parks.

Most of the materials used in this book are from the collections of the City of Spokane, Parks Department, held at the Eastern Regional Branch of the Washington State Archives in Cheney, Washington. Images are from the Washington State Archives collection unless otherwise noted.

Other images featured in this book are in the collections of the Northwest Museum of Arts and Culture (MAC) and the Spokane Public Library (SPL) and will be noted.

INTRODUCTION

The city of Spokane sits on the unceded traditional homelands of the four bands of the Spokane tribe of Indians: Sntút?ulixʷi, Snxʷmene?i, Scqesciłni, and Sčewíle? (Upper Band, Middle Band, Lower Band, and Chewelah Band). The Spokane tribe of Indians has lived and cared for these grounds covering approximately three million acres in northeastern Washington. For more information about the Spokane tribe, visit their archives.

Spokane was no different from the rest of the cities in the United States when it came to the parks movement. In many ways, Spokane's founding fathers were a little more forward-thinking than cities like New York, Boston, and Chicago, but in others, they struggled with similar issues. Spokane's 150,000 Club, part of the nationwide City Beautiful Movement, wanted to prove Spokane was a growing Western city, not just a boomtown. Club founder, park promoter, and environmental activist Aubrey L. White pushed the City of Spokane to acquire land before development rather than buy land when property values increased. The club reasoned parks would attract more settlers and long-term residents, and the City of Spokane's goal was to have a park within walking distance for everyone. White and several early builders of Spokane acquired land by donation, agreement, or handshake, only purchasing property when no other arrangement could be made. This practice helped Spokane at the time but proved to be challenging in later years.

The city of Spokane had parks before it officially had a park board and parks department. The earliest park was deeded to the city in 1891. Spokane's Public Works Department oversaw the city parks from 1891 to 1907. Early park papers are few, but the earliest invoices, plant lists, and correspondence date to 1896. E. Charles Balzer was an early park superintendent and lived in Manito Park. Earlier records may be found in the City of Spokane council minutes. The Spokane Board of Park Commissioners was officially established in 1910 and granted power by Article V of the city charter to lay out, establish, purchase, procure, accept, and have the care, management, control, and improvement of all parks grounds and parkways controlled by the City of Spokane and used for park purposes.

Though never a city park, Natatorium Park began as Twickenham Park, part of the Twickenham Addition North of downtown Spokane along the river. Natatorium Park would be a big part of Spokane's history from 1887 to 1968. The park went through many changes. Washington Water and Power had an interest in the park in the early days and hired park concessionaires to run the day-to-day operations if it did not cost them a lot of extra money. With dreams of making it the Spokane Coney Island, Audley Ingersoll leased the park from 1907 to 1908 and made major changes. It was this Coney Island vision that attracted Charles I.D. Looff and his hand-carved carousel to Natatorium Park. This gift to his son-in-law as a wedding present sparked the job of park concessionaire for Louis Vogel, and the park was sold to Louis Vogel in 1929. The Vogel family ran the park from 1929 to 1962, when the Spokane Park Board considered taking over but decided against it. The park was purchased by El Katif Shrine Temple and Shrine Park Association, but eventually, Natatorium Park was razed to the ground and the land became San Souci West, a residential trailer park.

The parks established in Spokane from 1907 to the late 1930s are examples of reform park design. Influenced by elements of contemporary social reform movements, designers of reform parks felt most people could not be trusted to manage their own recreation and configured the parks to provide structured enjoyment. Children needed organized play, and adult men needed something wholesome to take them away from other recreational activities such as drinking and gambling. Heavily influenced by the *Report of the Board of Park Commissioners*, released in 1913 with the recommendations of landscape architect John Charles Olmsted of the Olmsted Design firm in Massachusetts, Spokane concentrated on creating a series of large parks and smaller neighborhood parks with specific purpose funded by a $1-million bond that passed in 1910. The larger parks would have a combination of spaces for quiet reflection and recreational grounds, and smaller parks would cater to the neighborhoods. Newspaper articles encouraged residents to clean up their yards and green spaces, and the city took care of the parks. Examples of these early park designs included Coeur d'Alene, Manito, Liberty, Corbin, and Hays.

At the beginning of the 1930s, the needs of parkgoers changed. Park administrators abandoned the social reform movement of parks and instead created spaces for leisure. This recreation era provided playgrounds, playfields, parkways, stadiums, and entertainment options for the whole family. Spokane saw a demand in the requests for more park development. Residents noticed the empty green spaces and asked for tennis courts, playground equipment, and supervised play in their area. As this was the time of the Great Depression, Spokane took advantage of the many unemployed men in the area. The parks department was able to improve parks using programs such as the Works Progress Administration, the Civilian Conservation Corps, and the Washington Emergency Relief Administration. The public's (or people's) expectation of the city to provide space for recreation and leisure caused a surge in parks added, created, and/or redesigned from the late 1930s to the early 1970s. These parks were either created with recreational activities in mind like Comstock, Shadle, Nevada, and B.A. Clark or altered to reflect the surge in recreation like Mission, Grant, Liberty, and Lincoln.

In the open space system, or the "anything goes" period of park development beginning in 1965, the park grounds could be used for a multitude of purposes. Gone were the expectations of what a park should look like. Instead, park design incorporated anything and sometimes included earlier design elements of all kinds. Social class, race, inner city, and suburbia were all elements of this new discussion of parks and park use. For Spokane, this era began with a new push for a park bond in 1965 and the planning of Expo '74. Parks acquired after 1974 would go undesigned or left undeveloped until neighborhood groups decided what they would look like. Riverfront Park is an example of an "anything goes" design with its IMAX theater, trails for bikes and walkers, large green spaces for sunning and picnics, and concessionaire-driven rides. Large parks meant to conserve the Spokane area's natural beauty include spaces like Wyakin, Austin Ravine, Camp Sekani Conservation Area, Drumheller Springs, and Rimrock Conservation Area.

The comprehensive history of Spokane parks has yet to be written. This collection of park photographs is incomplete with many gaps, so the stories will be told in grouped themes. The photographs jump from 1910–1930 to the 1950s and then the 1970s with little to fill in the blanks. This is the story of the City of Spokane Parks and Recreation from its own records. There are many voices in this history that were not included. Additional research is necessary to discover how park development and settlement impacted the indigenous people of the land as well as how these development decisions impacted people of color.

One

PLAY

The early parks in Spokane were not all owned and operated by the Spokane Parks Department. This small collection of images showcases a few of those parks that started in the earliest days of Spokane's city development. One of the earliest mentions of a public park was in the *Spokane Falls Review* of Saturday, July 21, 1883: "A.M. Cannon and Mr. Brown will lay out a public park containing fifteen acres." They later offered to deed it to the city in 1887 as Coeur d'Alene Park, and finally, it became an official city park in 1891. People found green spaces in the Spokane area and places to entertain themselves whether they traveled to nearby Liberty Lake, the cemeteries, or the fairgrounds north of the city. Natatorium Park was never owned by the Spokane Parks Department, but it lives in the hearts of those who remember living, playing, and picnicking there. Some parks started as early ventures for Spokane's entrepreneurs. Francis H. Cook came to Spokane to seek his fortune and started by buying 680 acres of land. His gift to the city ended up being a park he named Montrose Park for the wild roses that grew in the area. He would not be the one to transfer the land to the city; his luck ran out and he lost much of his wealth in the Panic of 1893. Montrose Park would become Manito Park in 1904. Gifted to the city by the Spokane Washington Improvement Company, Spokane & Montrose Motor Company, Washington Water and Power Company, Hypotheekbank, and F.P. Hogan, the park contained 90 acres. Review Rock in Cliff Park and Hays Park were other early examples of development companies that donated parks to the city to entice homeowners to buy the land surrounding the park.

This bird's-eye view of Spokane Falls, Washington Territory, from 1884 features the falls in the center of town. It also shows a listing of churches, schools, manufactories, hotels, banks, leading business blocks, and business references. The view is facing south.

Cable cars, electric rail, and horse-drawn carriages were the various methods of transportation used to leave the dirty, dusty, hot city for cooler areas filled with trees, lawns, plants, and access to ponds, lakes, and the river. Many parks started as a destination positioned at the end of a streetcar line. People could ride for a small fee and enjoy the outdoors with entertainment that would cost extra.

An ad in the *Spokane Chronicle* dated Saturday, May 14, 1892, about Twickenham Park reads, "Easy access by the electric lines of the city. It lies over the hill just west of the ballpark on a picturesque piece of ground divided into three natural terraces. Picnic grounds, dancing pavilion with a bell stage at the north end, an artistic band stand for afternoon concerts, a bar disbursing the finest domestic and imported liquors and cigars. A fine restaurant is maintained under the supervision of an experienced chef." (SPL.)

Twickenham Park hosted annual picnics, baseball, and croquet and ladies serving luncheon from the First Baptist Church and the Mission Sunday School in 1890. Washington Water and Power (WWP) bought the park in 1893 and allowed various entrepreneurs to run it for the company until it was sold to Louis Vogel in 1929. According to the *Spokesman-Review* from September 8, 1907, Audley Ingersoll is known for transforming it into a Coney Island–style park. (SPL.)

On a hot summer's day, couples would stroll along the banks of the Spokane River to escape the heat and perhaps get a little closer than socially acceptable on Lover's Lane at Natatorium Park. The back of a picture postcard of this same scene reads, "His hand brushed against mine and my breath caught."

A bridge connected Fort George Wright to Natatorium Park so servicemen could enjoy the park and its various entertainments. Concerts, sporting events, and picnic areas in the early days gave way to rides, carnival games, a small zoo, and plenty of refreshments. Many Spokane residents have fond memories of the park.

Built in 1910, the Plunge Pool was an Olympic-sized swimming pool within Natatorium Park. Filled with well water, it had a domed roof and was surrounded by 300 changing rooms, each with its own window. The first pool, built in 1895, used river water and was boasted as the first heated pool in Washington.

This well-dressed crew was tasked with watching over the many patrons of the pool at Natatorium Park. It was their job to step in to save a life by throwing a rope or floatation device to the swimmer in distress. Occasionally, they would have to jump in and perform a rescue. (MAC.)

A girl reaches out for the brass ring on the Looff carousel. Louis Vogel came to Natatorium Park with his wife, Emma Looff, and the carousel. This hand-carved carousel was offered to WWP for $20,000 by its carver, Charles I.D. Looff. WWP was not willing to pay but did hire Vogel as the concession director, and the carousel was given to Vogel as a wedding present from his father-in-law-to-be.

Pictured here is the Dragon Slide, where riders climbed to the top and slid down, coming out the mouth of the dragon like fire. Natatorium Park was the place for rides in Spokane, but various concessionaires approached the parks department to request adding a ride or two in Manito Park or an entire children's amusement park in High Bridge Park. The parks department was careful not to compete with Natatorium Park. (MAC.)

Working in a midway could allow an employee to enjoy the concerts held at Natatorium Park without paying the price of admission. According to a former employee, Vogel preferred to hire young men from Fairchild Air Force Base (AFB). Games of chance, sugary snacks, and crowds of people walking from attraction to attraction kept people coming to the park to mingle and enjoy the festive atmosphere. (MAC.)

Ads for Natatorium Park ran in the newspaper as well as the city directories, atlases, and local travel maps featuring the major attractions in the Spokane area. Always free to enter, Natatorium Park allowed people to wander along the paths but tempted them to spend their money on the rides and attractions. Newspapers advertised (often a full-page ad) all the delicious treats from local stores and the entertainment offered at the park.

Pictured here is the Washington State Federation of Labor picnic in 1930. Natatorium Park hosted many picnics; some were for businesses in the area and others were large family reunions. The picnic brought people to the park, and after filling up on food, they could enjoy all that the park offered. Often, businesses would pay for their employees to enjoy some of the attractions as an incentive or in appreciation for a job well done. (MAC.)

Natatorium Park officially met its end when its roller coaster, the Jack Rabbit, was razed in 1968. Many of the other rides were sent to other parks or sold to interested individuals. The Rocket Ship Ride, part of the Circle Swing (1949–1968), now resides in Wallace, Idaho. The Rock-O-Plane was sold to an amusement park in Oregon. (MAC.)

This image shows Natatorium Park nestled along the Spokane River. Rides and attractions can be seen from this height. Notice the large parking lot, home for the carousel, the roller coaster, and the many attractions seen from the sky. The county assessor or State Department of Natural Resources periodically took aerial photographs to show land development, timberland, and changes in river flow. These can be used for habitat restoration, urban growth studies, and property history.

The 1909 carousel survived the closure of Natatorium Park and now sits at Riverfront Park along the Spokane River in downtown Spokane. Plans to include it in Spokane's World's Fair Expo '74 were discussed, but eventually, it was installed after the close of the fair in a building constructed for the expo. The carousel includes fifty-four horses, one giraffe, one tiger, two chariot benches, and a brass ring to catch.

The early entrance to the park included a hedge archway that proclaimed "See Spokane Shine" in flowers. This archway could be seen in many of the advertisements and postcards trying to attract people to the area. A trough for watering horses was at this entrance and can still be seen today. This pathway at Twentieth and Grand Avenues led back to E. Charles Balzer's home. Balzer was the city florist and early park superintendent. Early records with letters from Balzer list "E.C. Balzer, superintendent of city parks; Residence Manito Park." The letterhead also includes the list of the city parks. (SPL.)

Excited parkgoers witness a ball game on a sunny day on the South Hill in Manito Park. This field was slightly smaller than a standard ball field, but that did not deter from the enjoyment of watching a good game while enjoying an afternoon picnic. Grand Boulevard is to the right, and this may be close to where the hedge archway once stood. The path leads back to trees and a picnic area. (SPL.)

The pond at Manito Park once had a dance pavilion on one side and was used for skating in winter and bathing in summer. Early park superintendent Balzer recommended acquiring additional lands to run a canal or pipeline between this lake and the old brick kiln excavation site in the Adams tract in 1907 to help the water flow better between the two ponds and thereby avoid stagnant or swampy conditions. Long, hot, dry summers meant less fresh water to keep the pools clean.

Walking in the pines provided some shade and allowed city dwellers to get a taste of the great outdoors instead of traveling a far distance. This was only a trolley ride away and only a couple miles from downtown Spokane. Manito Park was also home to a zoo from 1905 to 1932. This zoo carried animals that city dwellers could see without traveling far from town.

Buffalo roamed the area now known as the Lilac Garden. Upkeep for the many animals was hard, and often neighbors would complain about the noise, the smell, or on the off chance one the animals got out, the chaos of trying to get the animal back and pay for any property damage. Many area businesses would donate or sell at reduced cost stale bread, older vegetables, and meat for the animals. (SPL.)

Elk could be seen grazing in the springs located where the Rose Garden is today. Animals who died in the zoo were sent to a taxidermist and donated to the Cheney Cowles Museum for display. In 1931, the year before the zoo closed, it had nine bears, four bobcats, four coyotes, seven deer, eight elk, twenty-eight mallard ducks, eight pheasants, three raccoons, one fox, one hawk, one emu, ten ring-necked doves, seventy pigeons, two golden eagles, one ostrich, three buffalo, two cougars, and two crows. It was difficult to get rid of the animals, as both the Washington State Department of Game and the US Department of Fish and Wildlife had restrictions on who could take animal donations.

The new greenhouses, located in Manito Park due to the valuable soil conditions, were built during the first part of 1912, making a comprehensive and complete range of houses both for the propagation of plants and for exhibition purposes. The greenhouses were purchased in 1912 from Lord and Burnham of Chicago for $20,000 and used to raise plants for the parks. They were heated by coal for many years.

This chrysanthemum display inside the greenhouse in Manito Park was planned by park superintendent John W. Duncan. He planned the shows in November, when the "mums" were at their best. Flower shows in winter showcased beautiful blooms and gave people something to look forward to in those long, cold winters.

Pictured is an example of an invoice from Vaughn Seed in 1907. While the parks worked with local plants, often they planted beautiful flowers to attract people to see the gardens. Park staff ordered plants from other places or traded plants with other city parks in Washington or Oregon. Often, the parks department took advantage of the agricultural focus at the state college in Pullman and called it for advice about plants and pests.

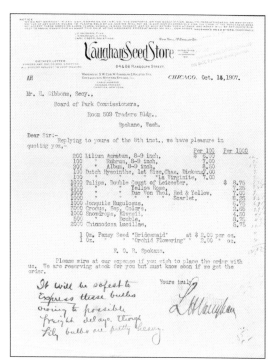

Pelargoniums are displayed in the greenhouse at Manito Park. The parks department used the greenhouses to keep plants alive during the winter and raise annuals for planting in the spring.

Parkgoers walk and bicycle on the paths through Coeur d'Alene Park. Concerns for safety were ever-present, as the advent of motorized vehicles tempted new car owners to drive on the paths. Signs were posted to keep out anything but pedestrians and bikes. (SPL.)

People enjoyed live music in Coeur D'Alene Park on Wednesday evenings in the summer. The neighborhood was filled with families mixed with boarders from many of the boarding homes in the area. The park board hired a band director for a certain number of shows throughout the summer. The band director was then tasked with hiring his band for the sum of money given at the beginning of the summer. (SPL.)

An early planting map shows winding paths through the park passing by a variety of trees, shrubs, and beds of flowers. The Pansy Garden included two large stone urns procured by a committee for the World's Fair in 1894. It requested the urns be erected in Coeur D'Alene Park.

Early park superintendent E.C. Balzer wrote to the board about improving the fountain in Coeur D'Alene Park by connecting to the city sewer line so unsightly and unhealthy water would not stagnate in the bottom of the fountain. He also suggested adding a cement bottom. Water features were a design element that was beautiful but challenging to maintain.

The tool shed was built in 1898. It also housed public restrooms and a place to store the tools needed to work on the park. Coeur d'Alene Park also was home to a greenhouse in the early days and housed a variety of plants to be kept in the winter. Some of those plants included 29 cacti, begonias, geraniums, silver oaks, water lilies, and dahlia roots.

Coeur d'Alene Park was home to some of the oldest and largest trees in the city. This was in part due to some of the trees planted, including varieties of poplar, pine, spruce, elm, chestnut, linden, maple, birch, and redwood, along with some ornamental fruit trees.

A basalt tower, once known as Review Rock, stands in Cliff Park. The park sits high on Spokane's South Hill on Thirteenth Avenue between Stevens and Grove Streets. Spokane is full of these large black outcroppings formed from molten lava rapidly cooling and forming these igneous rocks. Surrounded by homes and lawns, this rocky park seems to rise out of nowhere and gives a 360-degree view of Spokane and the surrounding area.

According to the park report, "This park is located on a rocky bluff, overlooking the city. With the work of grading and the planting of many thousands of trees and shrubs, with stretches of lawn intermingled among its natural rocks, the neighborhood is given a small park of most unusual natural beauty."

Hays Park, located between Providence and Gordon Avenues, was donated by the Big Bend Land Company to attract people to the area to buy property. In a 1909 letter to the park board, the land company stated it had concerns about its donation to the park board. The company had noticed no development in the park area and wanted to know when it could see a return on its investment. In 1911, trees and shrubs were planted with a rose garden at one end. A pathway went through the center of the park as part of Napa Street.

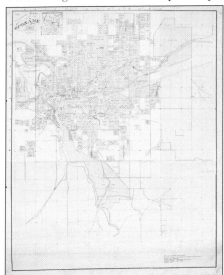

This map shows the parks in Spokane in 1907. Note the older names for parks including Queen Anne Park, Downriver Park, Gorge Park, Ravine Park, Adams Park (Cannon Park), West Heights Park, and Eastside Park (Upriver Park) and the plans for parkways and boulevards. This map shows the various bridges, buildings, steam railways, and electric and street railways that moved people from one part of the growing city to another.

Two

PLANNING

Planning Spokane's city parks was a monumental task. With the guidance of park promoter Aubrey L. White, Spokane Park Board Commissioners hired the Olmsted Brothers, famous landscape architects, in 1906 to review the park system and make recommendations. White found out they would be touring Seattle and Portland, and he requested they stop by on their way through. Initially, Spokane paid for the Olmsted Brothers to tour its parks and make recommendations for use of the land. A preliminary visit was anywhere from $50 to $500 depending on the importance or difficulty of the problem put before the firm. The visit fee was $100, and according to the invoice from the Olmsted Brothers, the visit in 1906 was $50. By 1912, Spokane would pay $5,499.16 for their initial visit, a report, and more specific plans for Liberty, Corbin, Adams (Cannon Hill), and Downriver Parkway. Correspondence included letters from John Charles Olmsted and James Frederick Dawson. The city received an introduction letter from the Olmsted Brothers for John W. Duncan, who became Spokane's park superintendent from 1910 to 1942. The *Report of the Board of Park Commissioners 1891–1913*, printed in 1914, included a short history of the parks and the Olmsted recommendations.

Liberty Park, located at the base of the South Hill between Arthur and Perry Streets, was deeded to the city in 1898. This park had challenges with its dramatic landscape of basalt cliffs and sprawling green spaces. The Olmsted Brothers noted the 24.5 acres are so broken into hills and valleys with abrupt slopes and prominent projecting ledges that the park is capable of uncommonly picturesque landscapes.

The early engineers fashioned wooden steps and structures to help navigate the landscape. Parkgoers could climb up and down the basalt rock via steps. The fears of falls and deaths were consistent during the years the park included the cliffs.

Putting lawns between the various levels of basalt added a landscaping design both beautiful and challenging for park employees. The park superintendent hired workers to build structures recommended by the Olmsted Brothers team. The wood structures deteriorated over time and required a lot of maintenance.

The Pergola and Summer House were recommended as shown in a topographical drawing. Behind the Summer House were a small wading pool and sandboxes for small children. The *Spokane Chronicle* on June 11, 1915, declared, "Liberty Park is the little children's playground. It has sand pits and a wading pool but no athletic field. There is no restriction as to age, but on crowded days the little children get the preference. Miss Henrietta Flournoy is the director."

THIRD AVENUE

ARTHUR STREET

FIFTH

LIBERTY PARK
SPOKANE · WASHINGTON
GRADING PLAN
SCALE 30′=1″

FILE Nº 3096
PLAN Nº 20 SHEET Nº 1

Landscape Architects
Brookline Mass May 18ᵗʰ 1909

OLMSTED BROTHERS
FEB 10 1910
BROOKLINE MASS

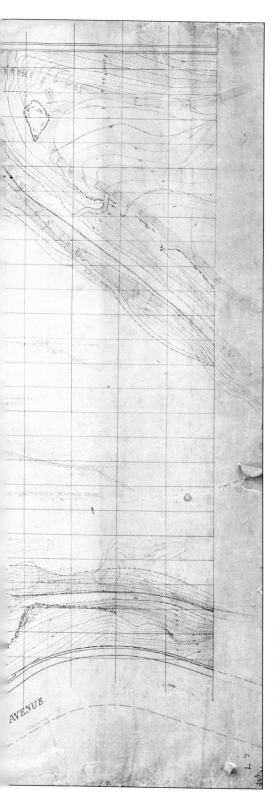

The Spokane Engineering Department was requested to draw the topography of the land and send the drawings to Boston for Olmsted Brothers to review and make notes. Shown in this drawing by the Olmsted Brothers is the topography of the area, including a sketch of the recommended structure built on the top of the basalt, using basalt as the pillars and adding in wood to form a pergola with porches and a promenade through the center. The ruins of this structure can still be seen from Interstate 90 Westbound right before the Trent Avenue interchange.

This structure stretched across one of the basalt outcroppings and included a wading pool and sandboxes behind so that mothers could stay close to their children while also enjoying the green grasses and flowered landscaping in front. A local company did the work with the plans provided by the park engineer, J. George Seupelt, and the Olmsted Brothers.

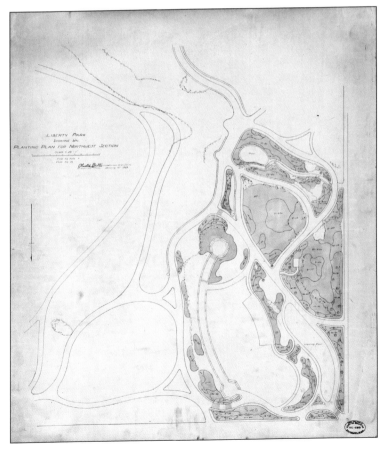

The Liberty Park planting plan, shown here, is numbered with the recommended plantings by the Olmsted Brothers. Varying heights of grasses, shrubbery, and flowers nestled in with the outcroppings of basalt made for a beautiful landscape. It is not certain how much of the planting recommendations were followed, but John W. Duncan, park superintendent and horticulturist, would have picked plants best suited for Spokane's climate and planting season over time.

A place to cool off, wading pools were almost as popular as the water features many modern parks use today. Children could splash and play while parents sat up the hill in the long basalt rock and wooden structure that gave a view of the surrounding area, Mount Spokane in the distance, and a little bit of peace. Surrounded by bushes and flowers, this was designed to help cool off during those hot Spokane summers to attract both adults and children to a place to escape the heat.

Laurence R. Hamblen, former park president, identified this lake in the park as an extinct volcanic crater. It was hard to preserve, and during the winter children would skate on it. The bottom was just muck, and the concern was someone would fall in and get stuck. Eventually, the park commission decided to fill it in.

The structure is seen looking northeast from the corner of Fifth Avenue and Arthur Street at the entrance to Liberty Park Playground. This land would later be used to construct Interstate 90. The parks department made an agreement with the state highway department based on the value of the land. The parks department was relieved to let go of some of the basalt areas that caused trouble with falls and potential dangers. The city received land from the state to redesign Liberty Park. (SPL.)

Cannon Hill Park is located on Lincoln Street between Eighteenth and Shoshone Avenues and was donated by the Adams Investment Company and the Cannon Hill Company. The park was originally called Adams Park and was part of the Adams Tract, an area developed into a neighborhood. Design recommendations included using the natural pool from the existing brick kiln and adding a shelter.

The Olmsted brothers recommended elm trees for the neighborhood but cautioned about the maintenance required to keep the trees healthy from pests or blight. They also listed low-growing bushes, such as the wild rose, Indian currant, and Japanese barberry to use along parkways to obscure the view of the road in residential areas.

The design for Cannon Park included a stone shelter, two pergolas, and a children's wading pool. The shallow pool easily froze and allowed for ice skating in the winter but kept children cool in summer. The smaller park was close to Manito, and the assumption was the park could stay quiet and refined so older children could walk to Manito for ball games and other sports.

Corbin Park is located between East and West Oval Streets at Waverly Place. Before 1899, this tranquil scene would have been filled with screams and yells from an excited crowd watching a horse race. The stadium, built in 1888, seated 1,000 and sat at the edge of a growing Spokane Falls. Corbin Park was home to the fair for at least one year, but in 1899, Daniel C. Corbin razed the stands and started platting the area for homes.

Daniel C. Corbin was an early Spokane businessman who dealt with mining and the railroads. The area surrounding the park was platted in 1899 as the Corbin Park Addition. Larger homes surrounded this park for many years, and residents felt like this was their own private park. The ladies in their summer finery and gentlemen in their hats and coats made a striking image. People sat on their porches to watch the who's who of Spokane walk in Corbin Park.

38

William Wallace Hyslop, an early Spokane architect, lived in one of the grand houses adjacent to Corbin Park and enjoyed the quiet neighborhood created by being on the edge of a park uniquely shaped as an oval. These children are enjoying a picnic in Corbin Park.

Hyslop children enjoy a game of croquet in their front yard with Corbin Park behind them. The park board would receive letters from parkgoers about the lack of organized children's play in Corbin Park. Anytime a recommendation for equipment would go before the park board, a petition of concerned citizens would request no park equipment be added.

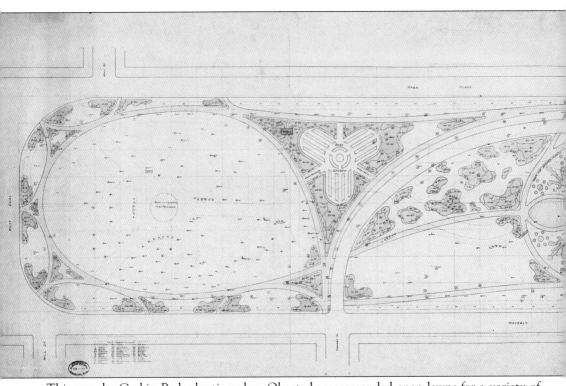

This was the Corbin Park planting plan. Olmsted recommended open lawns for a variety of recreational activities mixed with plenty of graveled walkways among flowers and shrubs. A mirror basin in the center and a small lily pond on one side were the only water features. In the *Report of the Park Board Commissioners, 1913*, the park had several shrubs with a couple of years' growth

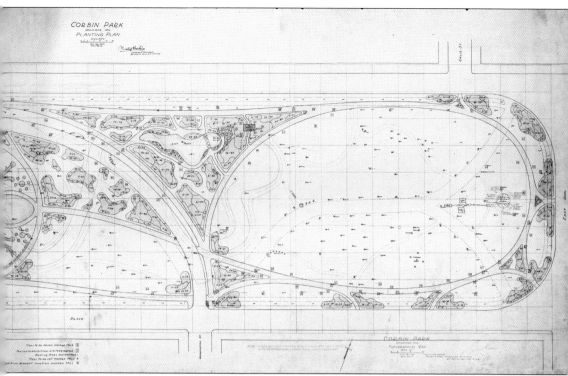

and two tennis courts enjoyed by many devotees of the game. Several elm trees were planted around the circumference of the park. The numbers on the plan corresponded to the different plantings, and lettered items note larger trees and shrubbery.

Corbin Park boasted a beautiful rose garden. Charles Uhden, a concerned citizen, wrote to the parks department in 1908, "I have noticed a few evenings that parties come into the Corbin Park and carry flowers away by the wholesale, mostly young girls, and in my opinion, something should be done to impress upon their minds the fact that this is not allowed." He concluded that he had no names but hoped the parks department would take preventative measures.

Some of the oldest shade trees in Spokane line the edges of Corbin Park. Concerns about the trees, their trimming, and upkeep were sent to the park board. The neighborhood loved its local park and did not wish for major changes. Strongly worded letters about the park board's plans for this space kept it free of children's play equipment until the late 1950s.

Three

PLAYGROUNDS, POOLS, AND PLAYFIELDS

The city of Spokane's parks included playgrounds, playfields, and pools. These elements were key to any successful park. Olmsted recommendations included recreation for all ages. As the parks developed, it became more and more important to make sure that each park had features to attract as many of Spokane's residents as possible to the parks and make them a big part of their day-to-day lives. Playgrounds started with supervised play. Play directors would be in the parks to assist children or adults with ways to play. Physical exercise was increasingly becoming important. It was up to the parks department to show people how to play. As the times changed, so did the offerings at the playgrounds. Organized play at scheduled times during the day or the week would have families coming. Pools gained in popularity as a place to come to learn how to swim and exercise. With the hot summers in Spokane, people enjoyed having a place to cool off. Some families could afford to leave the city and head to a lake, but for other families, this was not an option. Having a pool to take a streetcar to or walk to was easier and more economical. Some of these pools used heated water donated by the railroads. Playfields were designed for golf, baseball, and football, activities requiring open spaces to spread out but that needed additional grooming to separate the space from just an open field. The city had baseball leagues and created public golf courses so more people could enjoy the outdoors.

Manito Park Playground opened on July 27, 1913. Playgrounds included play supervisors to help children and adults with the ways of recreation. A man and a woman were stationed at four of the playgrounds from 10:00 a.m. to 10:00 p.m. daily. Two women covered the other two playgrounds from 12:00 p.m. to 8:00 p.m. (Liberty) and 10:00 a.m. to 6:00 p.m. (Manito).

Glass Park was one of the early playgrounds and boasted a play supervisor. B.A. Clark was hired to be a playground supervisor in 1916. When he went off to fight in France during World War I, his wife, Stella M. Clark, was employed to be the playground supervisor with a salary of $60 per month, and she lived in a building on the park grounds.

Formerly known as Chamberlain, the A.M. Cannon Playground was one of six supervised playgrounds in 1914. Playground supervisor B.A. Clark kept statistics on attendance and introduced new activities for parkgoers to enjoy. In 1915, he supervised a staff of six young men and five young women play directors. The first supervised season hosted 252,872 in attendance.

In 1920, Franklin Park Playground was added and became the eighth supervised playground. Many neighborhoods begged the park board to install equipment in all neighborhood parks. Often, citizens would form a group to raise funds and donate to the park board for equipment. Other times, equipment was reused in new areas. In 1920, the playground equipment was removed from the fairgrounds and placed at Underhill Park.

Here, at A.M. Cannon Playground, play directors teach children how to play to get the most out of it according to the *Spokane Chronicle* dated June 11, 1915. Anyone regardless of age was free to use any of the park apparatus subject to the classification that men are "boys" and women are "girls." A play director did not just referee—he saw children who were idle and showed them how to play a game of ball. Concerns about accidents prompted reports to the playground committee of the board of park commissioners. One in 1921 itemized the accidents that occurred while the grounds were supervised but noted no one could know what happened when not supervised.

Here in Manito Park, a few men enjoy a game of lawn bowling known as bocce (Italian) or *boules* (French), a game played by either teams or individuals. Parks were meant to appeal as much to adults as they did to children. Adults could spend some time in nature, socialize during a game, or exercise after a long work week.

Unidentified children pose in an unknown park on a jungle gym for an image used in a brochure advertising the Spokane Park and Recreation Foundation. Prominent businessmen urged the city council to approve the formation of the foundation to collect money or real estate to help with city parks maintenance, upkeep, and development.

Unidentified children pose in an unknown park on a slide. Images such as these were used in the promotion of parks. The park board passed a $1-million bond in May 1911 but had not been able to secure any additional large funding. Concerns about being able to keep up with the population growth of Spokane and providing plenty of parks had the park board finding ways to appeal to Spokane's citizens.

Children enjoy a trapeze swing in an unnamed park. Compare this with an earlier image, as this park apparatus continued in popularity from the 1920s to the 1950s. Imaginations soared as dreams of flying or circus performances danced in their heads.

Children navigate the rings with a carefully placed park bench in an unnamed park. Park supervisors had limited hours by the 1950s. In 1953, Audubon, Cannon, Comstock, Courtland, Franklin, Chief Garry, Glover, Grant, Harmon, Lincoln Heights, Lincoln, Manito, Mission, Shadle, and Underhill were supervised beginning April 27 from 4:00 p.m. to 8:00 p.m.

Swings were ever popular with children and adults alike. Notice the building in the background built with a stone facade. Many such buildings mimicked the earlier construction built during the Works Progress Administration (WPA) era in Spokane parks.

Boys enjoy a game of horseshoes, likely at Audubon Park, but the park is unnamed in the photograph. Junior horseshoes began in July, and a champion would be picked from each park to go to the playoffs at Manito Park in August. The schedule included an all–north side play day and an all–south side play day at Underhill Park.

Concentration is the name of the game as two unnamed boys challenge each other to a game of chess. This image was taken for use in a park brochure. Supervised activities included baseball, softball, tennis, and arts and crafts. The parks department consistently tried new things to draw people to the parks.

These children are enjoying a game of checkers with an audience. The pressure is on. Note the stack of checkers games on the table behind. Small games such as checkers, chess, and jacks were supervised at Comstock Park in the summer of 1953. Some of the play times coincided with swim meets—note the boy in the swimming trunks.

Children at an unnamed park enjoy a game of Ping-Pong or table tennis. There is an adult present to provide guidance on how to play the game and help other children join in the fun. Some parks had sheltered spaces for Ping-Pong and others set up tables under the trees. Note a couple of boys look like they have just come from a baseball game.

Girls enjoy a quiet game of checkers in Cowley Park. This small park named after an early Spokane pioneer is located on Division Street between Sixth and Seventh Streets. This small greenspace with a quiet creek is frequented by the doctors and nurses who work at the medical buildings in this area.

Dutch Jake's Place is located on Chestnut Street between College and Broadway Avenues. This park was dedicated in July 1976. Note the difference in design between the playgrounds in the early park history and this park with its wooden play structures and soft earth or wood shavings beneath the play area.

In 1924, Hillyard Pool was planned by the Hillyard Park Board with other interested parties, including the chamber of commerce. The City of Spokane answered the call for engineering assistance from one of the Spokane City engineers. The recently completed Liberty Park Pool was the inspiration for Hillyard's pool. Warm water was supplied by the Addison-Miller Icing Company, according to an article in the *Spokesman-Review* on May 20, 1924. The pool opened in 1925.

Wading pools such as the one pictured here were located at Cannon, Franklin, Glass, Liberty, Sinto, Underhill, Manito, Grant, and Lincoln Playgrounds in 1920. These pools included a supervisor but did not require a bathing suit, so often older kids and adults could be found enjoying these pools with their pant legs rolled up or holding up their dresses to a respectable level.

Sinto Park is a uniquely shaped park nestled against the Spokane River and the railroad. The bathhouse at Sinto Park was constructed in 1913, and a grand opening reception was held in July 1914. Trends for the time were to design spaces to include a wide range of parkgoers. Concern for youngsters' safety compelled the city to close parts of the road so children could come and go safely in the high-attendance summer months.

Comstock Bathhouse and Pool, at Twenty-Ninth Avenue and Howard Street, were the result of a generous donation from Josie C. Shadle in 1936 in memory of her parents, Mayor J.M. and Elizabeth Comstock. She included enough funds for the surrounding park and hired architects Whitehouse & Price to work with park superintendent John W. Duncan.

Mothers and children cool off on a hot summer day in Spokane at the Lincoln Heights wading pool. One hundred residents helped dig the space for the pool, and an event was created around the construction, as described in the *Spokesman-Review* of September 4, 1949. Neighborhoods could fund their own improvements by creating clubs that raised money.

Three unidentified children climb the rock at Comstock Park. The park included six tennis courts, four handball courts, athletic fields for football and baseball, and an open-air theater, as well as plenty of space for picnics and group gatherings.

Women and children cool off at the wading pool. Note the older style of the square pool. Many of these shallow pools would freeze in winter to allow for ice skating for younger children. As the upkeep became more challenging, the parks department would fill these shallow pools and install water features that merely sprayed water on a hot summer day.

An unidentified child slides into home plate at this neighborhood baseball game at one of the many playfields in Spokane. Playfields were a park design recommended by the Olmsted Brothers in their report in 1908. A playfield was a playground for outdoor athletics. Ideally, these places would allow for outdoor recreation in a designated spot, like soccer, baseball, golf, or football.

Early baseball games were supervised by play directors as there were enough children to play, but later, children were organized by different age groups into teams. Pictured here is the team sponsored by Looff's Food Market. Sponsorship helped with getting equipment and uniforms as well as advertisement for this business, located on the corner of Crestline Street and Empire Avenue.

Blodgett's Bears prepare to play a game. The city park league baseball program divided the teams into age groups. "Little Bears" were 8–10 years old, "Little Indians" were 10–12 years old, "Giants" were 12–14 years old, "Yanks" were 14–16 years old, and "Empire" included boys to 21. The game schedule would be released at the beginning of the season, and teams would play at various parks around Spokane in 1954.

A group of boys plays baseball at an unknown park. Ballgames were played on the south side at Lincoln Park, Garry, Comstock, Underhill, Lincoln Heights, and West Hills. Games on the north side were played at Franklin, Cannon, Audubon, Courtland, Shadle, Harmon, Rogers, and Mission in 1953.

The *Spokane Daily Chronicle* sponsored a pitching contest that included preliminaries in early May and a final held at Glover Field at the end of May. Pitchers had a pitching distance based on age. Targets had an opening two feet by four feet, and the bottom of the opening was eighteen inches above the ground. First- and second-place winners at the preliminaries competed in the final contest.

Baseball clinics or baseball schools were directed by Charles E. Canup, the athletic supervisor at the various parks, and a schedule was released early in the year. These clinics were usually held with assistance from the local minor-league baseball team, the Spokane Indians.

A man helps a boy holding the baseball bat while two other boys look on. This is representative of the baseball clinics or baseball schools held in Spokane to help boys improve their game. Parks hosted a two- to three-hour session, or the Spokane Indians held a free three-hour clinic at one of the parks and invited anyone interested to just show up. The minor-league team provided balls and bats.

Children line up holding their tennis rackets preparing to hit the ball. Tennis was a popular sport for many years. Parks started with asphalt or dirt courts and eventually had paved courts. Tennis was played in school sports as well as just for fun in the neighborhood park.

Sports were not limited to the able-bodied. Pictured here is a game for amputees at an unknown park. The Spokane Softball League included a team called the Amputees. The parks department received a thank-you note in 1966 from a family about a program for the handicapped held at Shadle Pool. It also received a letter in 1969 asking why the parks were not accessible to those in wheelchairs, as everyone wants to enjoy the parks.

Pictured are proud winners of the bicycle meet held at the Spokane Memorial Stadium. The meet included a safety demonstration and events such as quarter- and half-mile races, plank races, mile relay, and special races for regular racing bicycles. Boys were divided into Class A (16–18), Class B (13–15), and Class C (12 and under), and Class D was for girls of all ages.

Children enjoy riding their bicycles in a circle. It takes concentration to stay in a line and not collide with others. Bicycles were the most popular, but tricycles were also included for younger children.

This girl is navigating safety cones with a 10-speed bicycle. Safety demonstrations were given by a representative of the Spokane Police Department. Trophies and medals were furnished by the Bicycle Institute of America.

In 1953, girls' softball senior leagues played at Cannon, Courtland, Grant, Lincoln, Lincoln Heights, Manito, Shadle, Sinto, House of Good Shepherd, and Underhill Parks. The championship game for the seniors was played at Franklin Park on August 4. Park employee Mary Mele Mauro oversaw both the junior and senior leagues.

A girls' softball team poses at an unknown park. Note the onlookers behind the fence. The 1953 softball schedule was submitted with all the activities of the Spokane parks for 1953 to the Washington State Parks and Recreation Commission. The State Parks and Recreation Commission collected local park activities throughout the state starting in about 1946 for a statewide survey.

Adults were invited to enjoy recreational activities as well. Pictured here is the Downriver Golf Course, which was one of the first public golf courses in Spokane. The parks department hired a golf professional to oversee the season and provide training. Neil Christian, a Yakima golf pro, was hired in 1941 and was inducted into the Pacific Northwest Section of the Professional Golfers Association Hall of Fame in 1981.

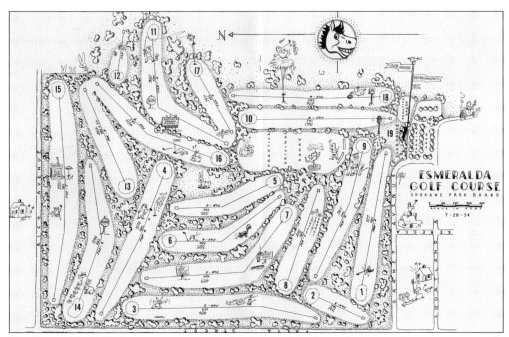

The Esmerelda Golf Course was constructed in 1956 in Northeast Spokane. This course was made possible by the Athletic Round Table, a club of sports boosters started in 1920. Spokane now had three public courses, including Downriver, the first public golf course, and Indian Canyon, designed in 1930 by Henry Chandler Egan, a golf architect, and built using Works Progress Administration labor.

Swimming, tennis, baseball, basketball, all competitive sports, arts and crafts, nature studies, skating and sledding in winter, Western dancing, and other activities are encouraged by supplying the means and providing leadership throughout the year. Games at parks continued to evolve and change as the times changed. A person is enjoying the Slip 'n Slide at an unknown park.

Sometimes organized play happened at a local park, and sometimes, children were bussed to a different area for the activity. Here, some children enjoy rock climbing at an unknown park. Rock-climbing routes existed at Minnehaha Park. Children would be bussed to Mount Spokane for skiing in winter.

Four

PICNICS AND PARTNERSHIPS

Many organizations, churches, neighborhood improvement groups, and chapters of national clubs approached the park board with requests to hold picnics, services, and gatherings of all kinds. The park board generated some income with its free parks by charging groups or asking for a portion of their fees or earnings to assist with the upkeep of the parks. The city of Spokane's parks' success was made possible through partnerships and community support. Over the years, the city partnered with Spokane School District No. 81, land developers, businessmen and entrepreneurs, the fairgrounds, the *Spokane Daily Chronicle*, and other cities working to grow and promote their parks and recreation departments. The City of Spokane Parks and Recreation Department was a member of the Amateur Athletic Union (AAU, founded in 1888) and tried to attend as many conferences as it could afford to keep abreast of new trends. It leased parkland to help generate revenue and offset maintenance costs. Several examples of this are covered in this chapter. There were so many ways these mutually beneficial partnerships helped the parks over the years, but not all of them are covered. Upriver Park leased land to early airline companies to assist with mail delivery, the war effort, and later private flying. Felts Field was the result of that early partnership with the parks. The park board was approached with many ideas, as seen through the records of the parks department; some of them never happened, and others are still part of the parks today.

Picnics were often a big event for parks. Pictured here is the setup for a picnic in Manito Park. The parks department would allow families, businesses, organizations, and churches to have gatherings, which could include picnics, activities, entertainment, and games. Depending on the organization, sometimes it would invite a speaker or have a full program as part of the festivities.

Picnics could be elaborate affairs. Note the china cups and saucers on some of the tables. Some groups brought their own food, while others used a catering service. Church groups usually had announcements in the paper inviting people to the event and, after, would recap who served and what was served at the picnic.

Entertainment was provided at most parks in the summer. This was the bandstand at Manito Park. At the beginning of summer, the park board would pay a band director a sum of money to put together a band and play in the parks. Band director F.L. Simmons was paid $3,018 to provide three concerts with 28 musicians for nine weeks in May 1919.

This image of a concert in Manito Park looks like a May Day festival with children holding hands and circling around several tall poles. Park benches were set up by park staff prior to the event. An article in the *Spokane Chronicle* dated August 9, 1915, describes a "Play Festival" to be put on in several parks with different themes—including one titled "A May Day Fantasy."

Going for a picnic was not always such an elaborate affair. This group sat on the ground on a cloth with food spread out in front of them. Note the tent to the left. While they were roughing it, they appear to be dressed in their Sunday best.

A family enjoys this picnic in the 1950s. A blanket was spread out on the ground with cookies, an orange drink, paper cups, and a few toys to entertain the children. This family found a piece of shade on a hot summer day to enjoy a family outing in Coeur d'Alene Park.

Often, family picnics were part of a church event. Notices in the paper announced where and when. Usually, the church provided things like ice cream, pop, and coffee and asked the families to bring their own basket lunches. Pictured here is a church group.

This group is concentrating on blowing up balloons. For large group picnics, the parks department provided activities for entertainment such as games, contests, croquet, badminton, or foot races. Sometimes, the groups supplied their own entertainment. Letters to the park board contain thank-you notes from various organizations, churches, and family reunion groups.

The stadium site on Main Avenue and Wright Street was 2.9 acres. Close to the center of the city in 1913, this was a perfect spot for events and gatherings. An athletic field with a six-lap running track was graded, and bleachers holding 10,000 people were erected. This proved the ideal location for athletic events, and according to the park report, the site needed to be enlarged by the purchase of additional property and filling in along the river.

The stadium site, later named Glover Field, was in Peaceful Valley, tucked against the Spokane River. Interschool athletic events were held at a cost of 25¢ per person with 10¢ going to the parks department for operating expenses. The parks department had an agreement with School District No. 81; the school district could use the stadium for only the price of upkeep and maintenance.

These boys are exercising at Glover Field. Note the Monroe Street Bridge in the background. In 1915, the Lewis and Clark football team moved its practice from Natatorium to Glover Field. The park board shied away from allowing political or religious gatherings in the public parks. Glover Field was different and was offered to any group that wanted to hold religious or political gatherings with the proviso that the groups paid for upkeep and maintenance after they were gone.

Boys play basketball at North Central. The parks department had a junior basketball league complete with a tournament. Rivalries between the north and south side of Spokane were usually intensely promoted before an event.

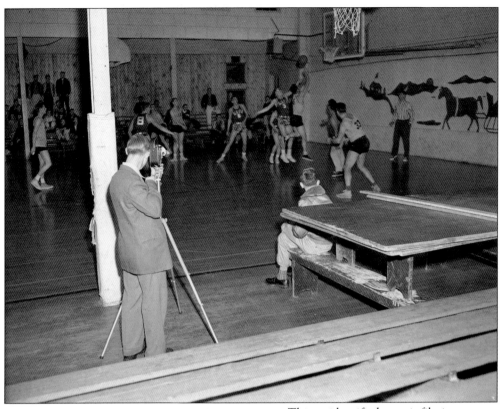

This unidentified man is filming a basketball game at an unknown school. A film was made for a variety of reasons; it could be shown to advertise basketball programs, provide training opportunities for playback, or air excerpts of a game on the local television station.

The boys stare anxiously to see if the ball will swoosh through the basket. Not all basketball programs were held at schools. During the summer, games would be played at various parks across the city. Most playoffs would be held at Underhill Park, located at Hartson Avenue between Fiske and Regal Streets.

Basketball moms wait for their children to finish playing in 1951. These women dressed in their evening finest to watch their boys play.

Lewis and Clark High School opened in 1912 and was located on Fourth Avenue between Washington and Stevens Streets at the base of the South Hill. The City of Spokane Parks and Recreation Department and School District No. 81 formed a partnership that benefited both the schools and the parks. Often, when a new school building was erected, the parks maintained the playground area next to the school. For a few years, the high school used the Spokane Interstate Fairgrounds as its athletic field.

Spokane city teachers enjoy an In-Service Day at one of Spokane's parks. In-Service Days usually occurred at the beginning of the school year and at the end of the school year as an opportunity to learn about new techniques and strategies for teaching and usually included a little fun.

The Spokane Moose Lodge staged Halloween parties in afternoons and evenings close to the holiday. According to the *Spokane Chronicle* dated October 29, 1953, there were 19,000 doughnuts and 800 gallons of cider. An estimated 13,000 children participated in these events.

These children filled glass containers with apple cider from a barrel for Halloween parties all over Spokane. Empire apple cider sold in glass jars at the grocery store for 45¢ a half gallon. Empire apples grew in the Yakima River valley, though apples also grew in areas around Spokane.

Dressed to scare, these children are ready to participate in Halloween festivities. This looks like a scene from a classroom but could have been a scene at one of the community centers in Spokane. Many of the area neighborhoods had betterment clubs that put on events for children like fall festivals, Easter egg hunts, and Fourth of July celebrations.

These well-dressed high school students are rehearsing for a movie called *The Dancing "Silver Spurs."* This 30-minute film, made in 1951 by Standard Oil and sponsored by Spokane Public Schools and the Spokane Park Board, was shown in Spokane in November. It made the *Journal of the American Association for Health Physical Fitness Recreation* January 1952 edition. This was a dream of E.S. "Red" Henderson who started the program in 1948. The dance troupe was featured in *Life* magazine on January 10, 1955.

Students performing in the film may have dressed this movie camera to lighten the mood. The group was made up of 18 couples. They learned dances from all over the world as well as traditional American dances like cowboy squares and ballroom dancing.

The Silver Spurs dance troupe was comprised of students in sixth through twelfth grade. Part of its appeal was the costumes, which were colorful and authentic to the type of dance they were performing. According to the Square Dance History Project, they took a 25-day tour in 1953, visiting 23 states and traveling 10,000 miles.

Dancing outside while the weather cooperates, they filmed on the South Hill, with the towering pines and Spokane cityscape in the distance. This may be the Glover Mansion. Square dancing was popular, and some of the parks had a dancing slab to host dances. Shadle Park had one installed and hosted the Washington State Folk Dance Federation festival.

Bicycle races at the fairgrounds were popular with boys of all ages. The fairgrounds were cared for by the City of Spokane. An ordinance passed in 1931 stated that "the City of Spokane has heretofore purchased and taken over the lands, buildings, and improvements formerly owned by the Spokane Interstate Fair."

Rounding the bend, one boy is clearly in the lead in a bicycle race at the fairgrounds. An announcement in the *Spokesman-Review*, dated June 8, 1951, stated "the annual bicycle races will be held at Playfair track June 16th." The races had different classes based on age and were divided into boys' races and girls' races; they also included a safety demonstration.

This is an advertisement for the Spokane Interstate Fair. The fairgrounds moved a couple of times in Spokane's history. When the fairgrounds were not being used for the fair or other large events, the park board answered requests from groups who wanted to use the space. The fairgrounds were listed as a lease to the City of Spokane in the Spokane Parks Report in 1913. The location at East Riverside Avenue and Lacey Street with 51.56 acres eventually became the location at the corner of North Havana Street and East Broadway Avenue. Grounds were improved to include a racetrack and an athletic field inside the racetrack perfect for athletic events. Requests to use the fairgrounds for polo, football, and sport shooting, just to name a few, came through the park board and were referred to the various committees for consideration.

The parks department partnered with the *Spokane Daily Chronicle* for many of the swimming and diving meets held at Comstock Pool. Pictured here is the 1959 swimming and diving meet held on July 30–31, 1959.

A diver jumps off the high dive in the pike position while onlookers sit behind the fence. Signs on the fence announce visitors from Kellogg and Multnomah. Comstock Pool hosted the Spokane Chronicle Swim Meet, which brought swimmers from as far away as Mexico.

Swimmers have just dived into the cool waters of Comstock Pool while men dressed in white watch the swimmers and keep time. A Spokane junior-age swim meet divided children into the following age groups: 10 years and under, freshmen (12 years and under), sophomores (14 years and under), and juniors (16 years and under). Swimming styles included freestyle, breaststroke, relays, and diving.

As swimmers dive into the pool to demonstrate technique, note the one diver who appears to be having second thoughts. Onlookers stand around the edge of Comstock Pool perhaps waiting for all swim. There were scheduled practice times so swimmers could practice before a meet. Swimming classes were offered at the city pools in partnership with the American Red Cross.

Minnehaha Park is located on Euclid Avenue and Havana Street. The land was once the summer home of Edgar J. Webster, a Spokane lawyer. John Heiber purchased the land from Webster and eventually donated the land to the Spokane Parks Board. This stone house has been the subject of much debate and still stands in the park. There were several buildings on the property when the parks department acquired it.

The park was formerly a private amusement park and had a dance hall. The parks department decided to lease some of the land to the Washington Motion Picture Corporation in 1917. The company added buildings to use as movie sets. The *Spokane Chronicle* ran short articles about the movie company's progress in Spokane. *Fool's Gold* was filmed in Spokane and taken to New York City but had difficulty with screenings due to the flu epidemic. It was released in 1919.

The articles of incorporation for the Washington Motion Picture Corporation were filed with the secretary of state's office in 1917. The purpose of the corporation was to engage in and carry on the business of making, producing, buying and selling, or otherwise disposing of moveable pictures, machines and films, photographic and optical goods, and similar machines. Movie sets were built at Minnehaha Park. Silent film star Nell Shipman came to Spokane in 1922 to shoot her film *The Grub Stake*. The Spokane Park Board continued to lease Minnehaha Park to film companies through the late 1920s. The film companies were to tear down their structures when they were done, but the sets were often left for the parks department to dismantle and remove.

No. 41611

Articles of Incorporation

OF THE

The Washington Motion Picture Corporation

Place of business Spokane

Time of existence 50 years.

Capital Stock, $ 500,000.00

State of Washington, ss.

Filed for record in the office, of the Secretary of State August 20th, 1917,

at 4.08 o'clock P. M.

Recorded in Book 113 Page 317

DOMESTIC CORPORATIONS

Secretary of State.

(FILE No. 21794)

Filed at request of ,
Zent & Povell
808 Sherwood Building,
Spokane, Washington.
Address

Filing and recording fee, $ 25.00

License to June 30, 1918, $ 15.00

(RECEPTION No. 172014)

Certificate mailed
OCT 6 - 1917 to above address.

INDEXED. Compared.

SS Form 47—4-21-17—5000.

A group of campers poses at High Bridge Park in 1927. Visitors came to the area from all over the United States. High Bridge Tourist Camp was meant for those traveling on a dime. It welcomed motor campers, tent campers, or those who slept in their cars. Park uses increased in the 1930s, and facilities like laundry and showers were added. Old oil drums were used as camp heaters.

High Bridge Park was located on Coeur D'Alene Street between A Street and Tenth Avenue and included 53.18 acres. The auto park was managed by C.B. Durant on a trial basis from the early 1920s to 1934, when he agreed to keep it up on a more permanent basis. He ran the camp until 1955.

This sign stood at the entrance to High Bridge Tourist Camp in the 1930s. The sign advertised to travelers all the sites to see, highlighting the parks and playgrounds in Spokane as well as many other sites in the Inland Northwest.

These children pose with their dog at High Bridge Tourist Camp. Note the drive and variety of camping equipment in the background. This camp and others like it were very economical for larger families who wanted to travel but could not afford hotels or motels. Some families preferred the nights under the stars.

This retired locomotive engine from 1904 is being hauled from the East Spokane Union Pacific railyards to its new home at High Bridge Park in 1955. The display site was prepared by the West Spokane Kiwanis Club according to an April 20, 1955, article in the *Spokane Chronicle*.

Maneuvering this large engine through town was not a small task. The trucks carrying this gift to the City of Spokane had motorcycle escorts and passed under one of the railroad's bridges this engine had crossed over during its useful life. The engine was transported from Portland to Spokane with the help of the railroad.

The 50-year-old, high-wheeled Union Pacific locomotive 3206 was placed in High Bridge Park with a wooden platform so parkgoers could look at the retired engine. A dedication ceremony was held on May 14, 1955, and it included former engineers. This engine now sits at the Spokane Interstate Fairgrounds.

The Wilbur Girls visit the conservatory at Manito Park. Various garden clubs and women's clubs traveled from surrounding towns to view the gardens.

Marble tournaments were a joint venture with the Veterans of Foreign Wars District 9. Boys under the age of 15 would compete in a citywide tournament, and finalists would go to the district tournament and, depending on their success, a national tournament.

This young man is getting ready for a winning shot. Marbles is a game played by drawing a three-foot-diameter, inch-thick circle and then choosing a shooter marble. Players then put 10 to 15 marbles in the center of the circle and use the shooter marble to knock the marbles in the center outside of the circle. Usually, the player who knocks out the most marbles wins.

These boys seem distracted by something, but one is getting ready for his shot. Marble tournaments were hosted at Comstock, Manito, Lincoln Heights, Lincoln, Underhill, Grant, Mission, Chief Garry, Franklin, Harmon, Glass, Audubon, Shadle, A.M. Cannon, and Courtland Playgrounds.

The Junior Lilac Parade was a joint venture between the Spokane Junior Chamber of Commerce, the Spokane City and County Recreation Departments, and usually thousands of children who participated in the festivities leading up to the parade. This is one event during a week-long Lilac Festival.

This was the staging area for the Junior Lilac Parade at Glover Field. The children, usually ages 6 to 14, assembled at Riverside between Monroe and Jefferson Streets to take place in some preliminary events including some judging for best float, best costume, and other awards before the parade began. A detail included in the *Spokane Chronicle* of May 7, 1954, was that the theme was "Vacation Is Grand in a Fairy-Tale Land."

The Junior Lilac Parade passes by the Fox Theater on West Sprague Avenue. The Fox Theater is an Art Deco–style building that opened on September 3, 1931, and showed films for many years.

A Washington Water and Power float passes by Firestone Tires on First Avenue. Crowds lined the streets while others took advantage of businesses' second floors for a good view of the parade.

The Centennial Flouring Mills float passes Nelson's Jewelers on Riverside Avenue. The Junior Lilac Parade in 1953 included elaborate floats celebrating Washington's territorial centennial.

The Spokane Park Board received several requests from a variety of religious, political, and labor organizations to meet in the parks or hold regular meetings, services, revivals, or Bible schools. For many years, the park board decided to discourage any such meetings. It would allow picnics but no reoccurring meetings. The groups were offered Glover Field or the fairgrounds if those were not already booked.

While religious services, revivals, and labor gatherings were not typically allowed in any of the parks, the Spokane Park Board decided to host sunrise Easter services in Shadle Park, Audubon Park, Manito Park, and later in Liberty Park. The early-morning services were open to the public regardless of religious affiliation. This image was captured during Easter services in Shadle Park in 1954.

Five

PRESERVATION

Creating a large park system was not always easy. The Spokane Park Board recruited interested community members to make decisions about the parks. Seasonal changes meant the park properties needed constant care. Showing the community that the parks added value to the city was consistently a concern. Petitions, suggestions, and lawsuits, as well as thank-yous, praise, and accolades poured into the parks department. The parks department struggled at times to keep up with the various demands and the financial cost of maintaining the parks. Keeping the city interested in the parks and how they helped people was a full-time job. Staff kept statistics on visitation, wrote articles and notes in the newspaper, and visited the parks to make sure things were going smoothly both visually and mechanically. When visiting a park, it is sometimes hard to see what work goes into the groomed lawns and beautiful gardens. This set of images showcases the behind-the-scenes of running a parks department.

The Spokane Park Board hosted an annual tour of parks each summer. It invited city and county commissioners, parks department staff, tourism staff, members of the press, and city officials. The 1950 roster had 41 attendees. The route and schedule were created ahead of time and often included a caravan of cars. Participants received official invitations, an itinerary, transportation, and lunch. This was an all-day affair to highlight successes and areas where improvements were needed.

Park board commissioner Louis M. Davenport spent most of his years on the board hosting the park tour at the Davenport Hotel or catering the park tour picnic using food from his hotel. The June 1916 park board report gave Commissioner Davenport a vote of thanks for the complimentary luncheon given on the general inspection trip of the board in June. Later, hotel owner and park commissioner Victor Dessert catered. Many of these were hosted in Manito Park, though on occasion, they would meet at Indian Canyon Golf Course or one of the larger parks.

This business card of the board of park commissioners from 1956 includes the standing committees. Board commissioners served on the committee that appealed to them the most, and many served on more than one. The committees were Improvement; Finance; Location, Designation, Acquisition of Grounds; Public Relations; Horticulture; Sports and Tournaments; Ways and Means; Recreation; and Privileges and Entertainment.

While many of the parks had landscaping that required little to no maintenance, each year, several parks had flowerbeds filled with plants from the parks department's nurseries. When attempting a park bond in 1956, the park board requested money for a park nursery at the arboretum and money to help rebuild and add to the Manito Park greenhouses to keep up with the plants needed for the parks.

This Adams Motor Grader No. 550 ran on diesel and made moving dirt a lot easier. It seems the park employees moved a lot of dirt in both the grading of park roads and to flatten ground for the development of recreational areas.

The caption on this undated negative reads "Park Apparatus Sand Rake." Children drag a large wooden rake used to remove debris from the playfields; the rakes were also used at the golf courses to clear debris from the sand traps. It is unclear if this was something children played with or just some park employee getting some help with the "cool tool."

This unidentified park employee locates the baseball equipment and gets it ready for spring play. This photograph, taken in 1951, shows the storage room for the baseball equipment for the Spokane Parks Department. Spokane Parks and Recreation hosted baseball leagues in several of the parks and provided equipment for play.

This unidentified park employee uses a sand rake to prepare the baseball field for play. The rake helped smooth out any divots, molehills, or other unseen hazards in the dirt. Much of the preparation was done as soon as the winter snow melted, which was very close to the playing season.

Park employees enjoyed the switch from push mowers to riding mowers. One mower shown here is receiving its yearly maintenance getting things ready for a spring season of care and tending to the city parks. Some equipment could be stored in the tool sheds often attached to the bathroom buildings. Equipment was also stored in larger garages, and employees used trucks to transport tools.

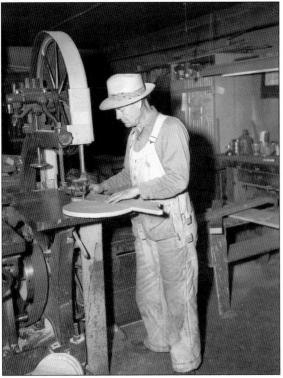

A park employee uses the bandsaw to cut pieces of wood or metal to build or repair park benches and other park equipment. The parks department did routine maintenance each year but had to contend with park vandals who would do damage to park buildings, furniture, equipment, plantings, and lawns.

This is the maintenance garage used to store park equipment at Manito Park off Tekoa Street in the 1950s. Some parks had enough space to hold smaller equipment and tools so employees could work with them onsite. Larger equipment was kept in these garages.

Park employees use this front-end loader to move and place cement barriers for the edges of the park to prevent driving on or trampling of the grass by other motorized vehicles. These were often moved during the winter season by snowplows and needed to be replaced.

Spring work included getting the tennis courts ready for play. School teams relied on the parks' courts to help give students the opportunity to practice. In the early 1920s, complaints poured into the park board requesting that more of the courts be paved rather than with gravel surfaces to help produce better tennis players. By 1951, most of the courts were paved.

The Spokane Parks and Recreation Department stored park benches during the winter to avoid excessive wear and tear. Other cities and organizations would inquire about leasing or renting park benches or bleachers for various gatherings. Spokane's park benches traveled to neighboring towns like Ritzville, Pullman, and Wilbur for different events.

Park employees paint the lines on the pool in preparation for the coming swim season. Pool lines help swimmers stay in their own lane. This 1951 image was most likely taken at the Comstock Pool. Much of the swimming competitions were held at the Comstock Pool due to its size and the size of the surrounding park to accommodate families of the swimmers.

Outdoor play was popular in Spokane during the winter. Park crews cleared the newly fallen snow off the pond so children could enjoy ice skating during the winter months. Large metal cans were filled with wood to keep cold hands warm while taking a break from the ice.

Spokane children loved their snow days. Each year, the park board would announce which hilly roads would be closed for coasting (sledding). In 1936, the park board petitioned the city council for an emergency appropriation of $3,000 because of the unusually long coasting and skating season.

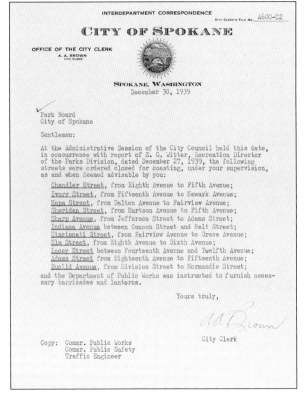

A coasting (sledding) hill announcement from December 30, 1939, names the street closures during the winter. The Spokane Public Works Department provided barricades and lanterns for the 11 street closures. Each year, the city council approved the closing of certain streets for coasting under Spokane Parks and Recreation's supervision.

In 1912, the commissioner of public safety received a letter from Dr. E. Pittwood requesting that the city council find some way of disposing of the "unsightly shacks" on Coeur d'Alene Avenue at the south entrance of the park along the Spokane River. He went on to say that the land was parkland (most likely today's People's Park) and that the park board should do something about it.

The City of Spokane partnered with the local health district to try and help disperse squatters who built homemade housing along the Spokane River between the Monroe Street Bridge and what is now called People's Park. During the Depression, camps were set up in Garden Springs, High Bridge, Downriver, and Seven Mile for men and boys who were out of work and needed jobs. They were put to work on several public works projects in the area.

In 1947, the park board of commissioners began to receive letters from concerned citizens about the condition of the trees in Franklin Park and the surrounding area. The board was familiar with treating trees for blight and pests, but this seemed different. Harold T. Abbott, one of the park commissioners, contacted the State College of Washington to assist with the problem.

On October 19, 1948, Abbott received a response from the college that the damage looked to be fluorine damage caused by the local aluminum plant, Kaiser Aluminum. Samples had been taken from Manito Park (8 miles south), near a gasoline factory (1.5 miles south), Franklin Park (4 miles southwest), and just south of the factory (500 feet). There had also been a scale problem but that had diminished while the trees continued to suffer.

City commissioners authorized the park board to find someone to remove 900 diseased trees from Franklin Park. According to the *Spokane Chronicle*, on January 6, 1950, the work was done by C.C. Weipert for $1,867, as it was the lowest bid received. Property owners who wrote the park board about the trees waited until the park acted before taking care of their residential trees.

The parks department received two payments from Kaiser Aluminum and Chemical Corporation to be spent on the rehabilitation of Franklin Park. The damage to the pines in Franklin Park was allegedly caused by fumes from the Kaiser Mead plant. The park board received a petition signed by 4,052 persons requesting the money go fully to Franklin Park.

This shows a speed limit sign in Franklin Park in 1949. Note the speed limit is 20 miles per hour. The parks department had to post signs in the parks with roads that went through them to remind drivers to slow down. Letters to the parks department reminded it children were ever in danger from speeding cars.

for You and for Generations to Come . . .

SPOKANE'S
PARKS AND RECREATION SYSTEM

In an attempt to raise funds, the park board commissioners were always on the lookout for ways to promote the parks and supplement their small budget with additional money. Prominent businessmen urged the city council to approve the formation of a foundation to collect money or real estate to help with city park maintenance, upkeep, and development. Many of the playground photographs from the 1950s were included in this brochure.

Six

PROGRESS

It was always the Spokane River. From the *Report of the Board of Park Commissioners, 1891–1913* through today, the importance of the Spokane River being a force that draws people to Spokane and the surrounding natural beauty is apparent. The natural beauty of the area was both a help and a hindrance. Natural resources from these spaces were used to build in and around Spokane. The power of the river was covered in train tracks and bridges. As the parks department evolved and grew with the times, the importance of protecting these natural spaces became clear. Aubrey L. White, a park board commissioner, recommended the Deep Creek Canyon and Riverside Park areas be transferred to the budding Washington State Parks and Recreation Commission. The parks department took advantage of the help provided during the Depression and had camps along the river for men and boys looking for work. The wild spaces became places for the US military to set up housing during World War II. This would all fade away to an urgency to acquire more land along the river to showcase its beauty and power, help with erosion, and set aside places for the conservation and preservation of natural flora and fauna. Spokane's love affair with Natatorium Park would be renewed with Riverfront Park's concessions and rides in the center of the city with the falls as a major feature, and there would be a permanent home for the Looff carousel right in the center.

The focus was on the river during early settlement. This map from 1899 shows the potential of this budding city. Spokane was incorporated in 1881 as Spokan Falls with 350 residents. In 1883, the City of Spokane Falls changed the spelling, adding an "e" to the end of Spokane. In 1891, "Falls" was dropped from the name. Developers wanted to entice more settlers to create a city—the biggest city west of Minneapolis. The focus of this map is on the different industries in and around Spokane, which includes agriculture, mining, logging, and oil reserves.

This is the view looking north from Latah Valley. This area of Spokane was known for farming and contained a rich river valley. Many of the farms along the Latah Creek fed the early city of Spokane. Later, a variety of nurseries and farms continued to benefit from the flood plains of the creek. The bluffs above were noticed by the Olmsted Brothers, and they recommended a drive to enjoy these views, which became High Drive.

High Drive travels along the ridgeline directly above the Latah Valley. Drivers can look west to see the ridge on the other side of the valley. Spokane has several scenic byways that connect the city to the outdoors over a short distance.

Hikes were part of supervised play and were considered an activity. The hikes were more than a simple walk. One hiking route began at the end of the North Howard streetcar line and went to Dartford and back, about 12–14 miles round-trip. According to the *Spokane Chronicle* on June 11, 1915, the hike was a great institution of playground life. "It is a joyful event to be looked forward to for weeks. It is a reward of merit and a mark of honor. Supervisor Clark leads the hikes for the boys and Miss Hardin those for the girls."

Climbing the tall basalt cliffs is not for the faint of heart. This woman is standing high on top of a basalt pillar in the Deep Creek area along the Spokane River. People enjoyed exploring the various natural areas along the river. This image was captured by famed Spokane photographer Frank Palmer.

In this photograph taken by Frank Palmer, a woman has climbed to the top of this basalt tower with a companion. The Deep Creek area has several trails that include a canyon, a wooded forest, and large areas of lava rock.

Hiking along the Spokane River was a pastime shared by many over the years. According to the *Spokane Chronicle* on April 24, 1920, a group of 100 freshman girls of Lewis and Clark High School were the guests of the Girls' Athletic Club and hiked in Downriver Park. This outing included a playlet, *A Midsummer Night's Dream*, and roasting hot dogs on a bonfire.

This group is taking a moment to stop and rest along the trail. The parks department had hiking events and a few outdoor clubs in Spokane that also encouraged people to get outside and hike. This photograph is probably of the Spokane Mountaineers Club, founded in 1915 as an all-women's group and originally called the Spokane Walking Club. In 1921, the group changed its name, and it allowed men to join in 1916.

Seen here is a trail through Indian Canyon, located west of Spokane in an area where the Spokane tribe camped until the 1920s. Local teacher E.T. Becher of Rogers High School brought his students there in the late 1950s to show a sign commemorating where Chief Spokan Garry was said to have lived. They noticed the sign was in poor condition and asked to replace the monument.

Chief Spokan Garry was said to have lived close to these falls in Indian Canyon. A sign was placed in his memory that states, "1811–1891 Spokan Garry Born to a chief and orphaned at 11. Garry was taught by missionaries to aid in fur trading. He was a teacher, a leader, a hunter, and a peacemaker. Always the white man's friend, he was refused citizenship, burned off his land, deprived of his earthly goods and finally his dignity by the white man. He died here a lonely unwanted person in the land of his birth and the land he loved. Garry and his wife, Nina, are buried in Greenwood Cemetery."

Indian Canyon Gulch is part of a larger park called Palisades Park. This park had resources used in the building and construction of Spokane. The board of park commissioners minutes mention requests for the city and for individuals to take rock and sand out of the area to use in projects, especially during the Great Depression.

The Spokane Bird Club members wrote the park superintendent, John W. Duncan, in 1935 over their growing concern that as Spokane expands, there are fewer spaces for songbirds to thrive. The letter goes on to say construction in the areas around Spokane endangers species. They requested a bird sanctuary be set aside in Manito Park around the old elk pond, upper Indian Canyon, and Garden Springs, which was already home to the long-tailed chat, the willow thrush, the red-start, the lazuli bunting, and the winter wren.

The park board granted permission to the State Highway Commission to remove rock for highway construction purposes from the Palisades Park area, east of Rim Rock Drive, under the supervision of the park superintendent on the condition the place where the rock was removed was left in a "sightly" condition in 1933.

The park board granted permission to Col. F.G. Knabenshue to remove rustic rock from Rim Rock Drive for the construction of a chapel at Fort Wright in February 1934.

On October 25, 1934, a resolution adopted by the park board was given to the city council recommending it deed Downriver Drive and Deep Creek Canyon Park to the state to be taken over as part of the state park system. This included the driveway just below Downriver Golf Course on the north side of the river extending to Seven Mile Bridge and then across down the south side of the river near Fort George Wright.

Bowl and Pitcher are named for the basaltic rock formations along the Spokane River that look very similar to a pitcher with a bowl lying on its side. This was once part of Deep Creek Canyon Park and is now part of Riverside State Park. The dark rocks are Columbia River basalt lava flows.

In an article written by Aubrey L. White in the *Spokesman-Review*, published on March 20, 1938, he recounts how Riverside State Park evolved over the last 10 years. He gives credit to the combined efforts of the Spokane Parkways Association, officers and directors of Washington Water and Power, the US Forestry officials, the National Parks Service, and W.G. Weigle, the superintendent of state parks. Much of the work was completed by the Civilian Conservation Corps camped at Seven Mile.

Aubrey L. White Parkway was named for the former park board president (1907–1922) and champion of the Spokane parks. In his own works, "early parks were a little more than groves where the citizens might picnic on a holiday . . . nobody expected more of the park than space, shade, and a cool breeze now and then . . . we campaigned the city, showing the actual value of the parks, pointing out the desirability of playgrounds situated within walking distance of every Spokane home."

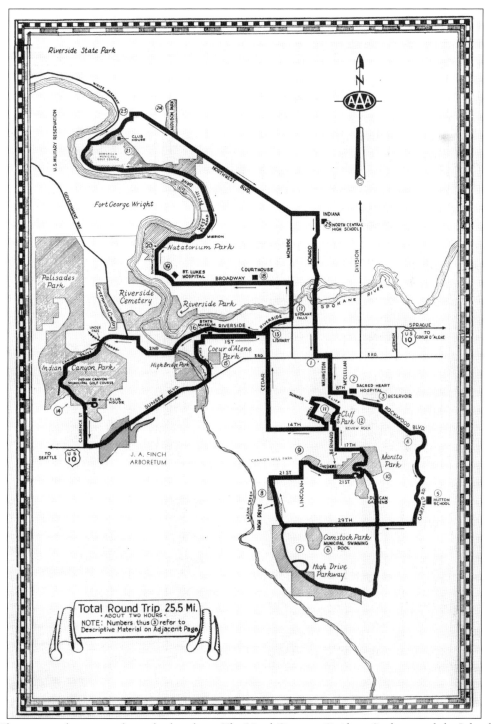

This scenic drive map from the brochure *The Hotel Greeters Guide to Spokane and the Inland Empire* from 1948 showcases the best of the best when it comes to the beautiful places to visit while in Spokane. Created to entice visitors to come to Spokane and check out the surrounding area, this map highlights several of Spokane's city parks and parkways.

Garden Springs Park was located on Spring Street, between H and Twelfth Streets; it had been purchased and included 35.11 acres. John A Finch, a local businessman and mining company magnate, donated the rest of the land in this area, which grew to include 65 acres of wooded hills. This stretch of land would eventually become the John A. Finch Arboretum.

In 1948, a letter to the Public Housing Administration notified the organization that the park board was moving forward on developing an arboretum and asked when the housing would be removed. The administration started with Block 13, Queen Anne Addition. The State Highway Department had also used a portion of the land for a sand storage bunker and a gasoline storage and greasing shed, all to be a temporary solution. The park board requested the highway department remove the installations by April 1, 1948.

In July 1940, the Spokane County Health Department wrote the park board to request permission to use a building at the old transient camp in Garden Springs Park. The county and state health departments were joint sponsors for a Works Progress Administration project for the construction of US Public Health Service Sanitary Privies and were required to provide a site for the work to be done. In October 1940, they wrote to say never mind and regrets for any inconvenience.

Stanley Witter and the city recreation department included science and industrial trips for boys and girls in grades fifth through eighth. The trips included observations of the big bombers at Fairchild Air Force Base, geological history at Deep Creek Canyon, seeing paper made at a paper mill, and learning about plants, insects, and reptiles at the Finch Arboretum.

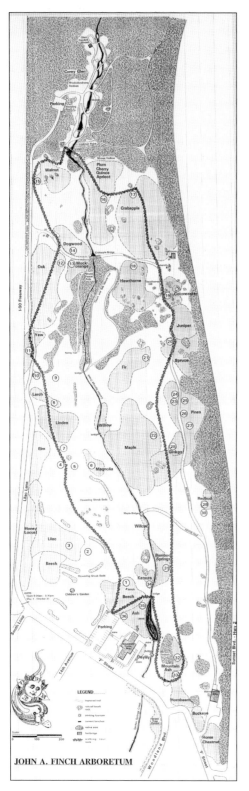

JOHN A. FINCH ARBORETUM

Finch Arboretum is located between Sunset Boulevard and Interstate 90. This map of the layout of Finch Arboretum gives the various plantings and features of the park. The Touch and See Nature Trail was added in 1972. The 850-foot trail was designed to include the blind in the enjoyment of the arboretum. The nature trail includes braille signs, a cotton rope to guide, and plants. The park development was made possible by a sizeable trust fund donated by John A. Finch.

Park board members kept an eye on real estate in Downtown Spokane—anything close to the river and the falls. In one board meeting, the acquisitions group was asked to approach Sears, Roebuck and Co. to see if it would be interested in donating any of the land not being used along the river to the parks department.

This shows the erosion along the banks of the Spokane River in Downtown Spokane, where there is much development. Notice the train advertisement on the right-hand side of the photograph. Multiple train tracks zigzagged through the Downtown Spokane area, and many of them obscured the view of the river and covered the two islands in the river.

Montgomery Ward & Co., a large department store chain, owned property close to the river, and the park board discussed approaching it to see if it was willing to donate any of the land to the parks department. The railroad bridge is hiding the Washington Water and Power building adjacent to the Spokane Falls.

A view of the river east of Downtown Spokane shows the Mission Avenue Bridge. This area of the river was a little calmer, and development had stopped just shy of the riverbank on both sides.

Preparations for Expo '74 included taking a long look at the space closest to the Spokane River and the falls in the center of the city. It was this river and the falls that brought people to settle in the area. An environmental movement was emerging, taking seed in the 1940s, and now in the 1970s, people were more aware than ever of their impact on the environment.

The Olmsted Brothers recommended keeping the space along the river natural and wild. By the time the city was planning to host a world exposition fair, a visitor could barely make out the river through the industry that had grown up around it. This photograph shows the demolition of the various structures covering the view of the Spokane River and Falls.

This is a view of the Spokane River downtown in 1972. Many railroad bridges crisscrossed over the river, obscuring the view of the falls. (SPL.)

Note the before and after images of the Spokane Falls once the railroad bridge over the Spokane River was demolished. These images were taken by Jacob Dormaier before and during Expo '74 in Spokane. This collection is held by the Spokane Public Library. (SPL.)

This is a view from above the World's Fair Expo '74, held in Spokane from May 4 to November 3, 1974. Pres. Richard Nixon presided over the opening ceremony. Future president Jimmy Carter also made an appearance at the fair. Bridges still crossed the river, but the river was visible.

A couple of ducks glide over a calm pool with the Great Northern Railroad Depot clock tower in the background. Built in 1902, the depot was a three-story-tall brick building, and the clock tower stands at 155 feet. Havermale Island and Canada Island (Crystal Island, Cannon Island) split the river into a calm pool and the rushing rapids tumbling down rocks to the falls.

After Expo '74, Riverfront Park became Spokane's downtown park along the river. The park included wide open spaces for events and picnics. Many of the buildings for Expo '74 were torn down or repurposed, and the pavilion, shown here, became the place to enjoy amusements, sugary snacks, and rides.

The iconic downtown image of the train station clock tower is surrounded by large open greenspaces to enjoy a family picnic or catch some rays of the summer sun. The Looff carousel, once an attraction at Natatorium Park, found its home shown to the right just below the tower. In 2014, the carousel enjoys a climate-controlled space to ensure the longevity of the wood carvings.

BIBLIOGRAPHY

Bamonte, Tony, and Suzanne Schaeffer Bamonte. *Manito Park: A Reflection of Spokane's Past.* Spokane: Tornado Creek Publications, 1998.

———. *Spokane: Our Early History, Under All Is the Land.* Spokane: Tornado Creek Publications, 2011.

Cranz, Galen. *The Politics of Park Design: A History of Urban Parks in America.* Cambridge: Massachusetts Institute of Technology, 1982.

Fahey, John. "A.L. White, Champion of Urban Beauty." *Pacific Northwest Quarterly* 72, No. 4 (October 1981): 170–179, JSTOR.

———. *Inland Empire: D.C. Corbin and Spokane.* Seattle: University of Washington Press, 1965.

———. *Spokane River: Its Miles and Its History.* Spokane: Spokane Centennial Trail Committee, 1988.

Hyder, Marla L. and Donald R. Johnson. *Dear Old Nat . . . Spokane's Playground.* Spokane: *Nostalgia Magazine,* 2003.

Newspapers.com

Popejoy, Don, and Penny Hutten. *Early Spokane.* Charleston, SC: Arcadia Publishing, 2010.

Report of the Board of Park Commissioners, Spokane, Washington, 1891–1913. Revision by the Spokane Parks Foundation and the Northwest Museum of Arts and Culture. Spokane: Marquette Books, 2007.

Williamson, Jerrelene, Spokane Northwest Black Pioneers. *African Americans in Spokane.* Charleston, SC: Arcadia Publishing, 2010.

Woodward, Doris J. *Indomitable Francis H. Cook of Spokane.* Spokane: Tornado Creek Publications, 2010.

Youngs, J. William T. *The Fair and the Falls: Spokane's Expo '74.* Cheney: Eastern Washington University Press, 1996.

DISCOVER THOUSANDS OF LOCAL HISTORY BOOKS FEATURING MILLIONS OF VINTAGE IMAGES

Arcadia Publishing, the leading local history publisher in the United States, is committed to making history accessible and meaningful through publishing books that celebrate and preserve the heritage of America's people and places.

Find more books like this at
www.arcadiapublishing.com

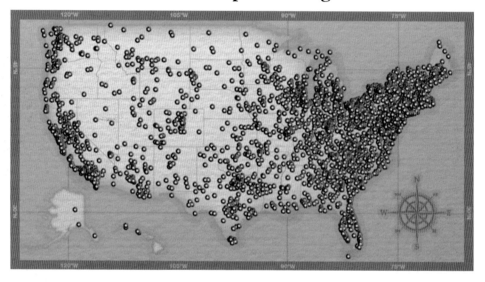

Search for your hometown history, your old stomping grounds, and even your favorite sports team.